CLEAN WATER IN FLOODS (WIF)

ANIK CHOWDHURY

Copyright © Anik Chowdhury
All Rights Reserved.

This Idea is dedicated to families who have lost their members in dangerous floods. We wish that this event was successful in spreading different family-level preparedness measures like this idea, water purification method, etc with the community. During these awareness projects, we hoped this will be a success in bringing community awareness on preparedness during a flood situation.

Flash floods swept through several towns in India after hours of exceptionally heavy rain, leaving hundreds of people dead and at least thousands got injured. Living with flooding is a natural part of life in places like Odisha. We can't prevent floods from happening, but we can take steps to be prepared by understanding our flood risk, where and how we get our flood warnings, and what steps we can take to reduce the impact of floods on our lives.

No two floods are the same and can vary depending on the quantity, duration, and location of rain falling on our catchments. But this idea will work in all types of floods,

Depending on your location, you may experience floods differently. Your location will determine whether you are likely to experience river, creek, overland flow, storm tide flooding or a combination of several of these types of flood risks. Understanding the type of flooding you are likely to experience will help you to prepare for how quickly the flooding is likely to occur, the duration of heightened flood water levels, where flooding is likely to occur, and the impact it will have on your home, workplace and transport networks. But, in which ever flood you experience, a person will always face the problem of clean water in floods.

Floods can cause containers of chemicals to move from their normal storage spots. This is why we need perfect sources of clean water in floods. Let's start

Contents

Foreword

I am delighted to write this foreword, not only because i am working for such a bright idea, but also because I believe deeply in the value of ideas for all people, especially in a democratic society.

I also believe that students at every level and stage of their career can enrich and strengthen their ideas by learning the problem solving patterns and practices presented in this book. Participating in interpretive discussions can help teachers and students alike learn to use their minds with power and pleasure.

The group introduced me to the concept of interpretive discussion when we worked together in the such a serious subject. Inspired by the Their teacher, garima ma'am approach to discussion that she encountered as a eighth-grade teacher, she taught her students how to prepare for and lead interpretive discussions of children's literature.

Students prepared clusters of questions and practiced leading discussions first with their peers and then with small groups of children in their practicum sites. As per my instruction, Ma'am has explored the students and practice of interpretive discussion through a dynamic program of scholarship and teacher education.

She has conceptualized the intellectual foundations of interpretive discussion, elaborated its distinctive pedagogy, studied its patterns and impact on teachers and students, and designed unique systems for inducting others xii Foreword into this powerful educational practice.

At the annual reunions of the school, I listened with admiration and interest as she described how she transformed her students to gold. Everybody should learn to teach like Garima ma'am, because brilliant teachers are not born , but they can be made.

Through this unique experience, scores of aspiring and practicing teachers were introduced to the power and practice of interpretive discussion that they, in turn, introduced to their students.

Anamika Chowdhury
Parent in kendriya vidyalaya, No-1

Preface

I realize that this book will create a great deal of problems. It has never been easy to challenge the consensus because the System – of any kind, in any context – will try to preserve the status , by all means possible. Hopefully, this book will raise the level of awareness among the general public and initiate the discussion that, in turn, may entail major cultural changes, as well as a revision of the needs in flooded areas.

The beneficiaries will be all of us – ourselves, our children, our beloved ones, the society, as a whole – who will live a healthier, and longer, life. I would like water consumption to be not a routine procedure for gaining clean water in floods, but a science-based process with complete predictability of its overall impact and fate of every water component entering the human body.

This book can be read on two different levels. First, it may be read by ordinary people with a limited, if any, scientific background. Throughout, the book has been written with this audience in mind. At times, the science presented might seem overwhelming: busy schemes with multiple structures. I hope that you won't be easily discouraged.

Even if the concept of a given book is hard to understand, the scientific evidence presented, the citations from original documents, conclusions drawn, and recommendations made can be easily comprehended. This book can be easily understood by a layperson.

One of the important features of this book is that it does not have a textbook structure when the chapters. I do not expect everybody in the scientific community to agree with the content and ideas put forth in this book.

But I do hope that the information and knowledge presented will become a wake-up call for the general public, regulatory agencies, legislators, business leaders, and scientists coming to the realization that the current state of affairs is not satisfactory, to say the least, and it needs to be fixed – urgently.

Acknowledgements

The world is a better place thanks to people who want to develop and lead others. What makes it even better are people who share the gift of their time to mentor future leaders. Thank you to everyone who strives to grow and help others grow.

To all the individuals I have had the opportunity to lead, be led by, or watch their leadership from afar, I want to say thank you for being the inspiration and foundation for The team.

Without the experiences and support from my peers and team at School, this idea would not exist. You have given me the opportunity to lead a great group of individuals—to be a leader of great leaders is a blessed place to be. Thank you to Ram Charan, Mashood, Hamood, Garima ma'am, and my enemies (because they play a serious role in motivating you.)

Having an idea and turning it into a really is as hard as it sounds. The experience is both internally challenging and rewarding. I especially want to thank the individuals that helped make this happen. Complete thanks to National science Congress

Garima ma'am, thank you for being a leader I trust, honor, and respect. I will always welcome the chance to represent you.

Chapter 1

It was a proud moment for all of us, when when we finally found a way to provide clean water in floods, the first one ever to successfully idea we thought. Why Floods? What makes this country more special than our other neighbors in the earth? What do we hope to learn from exploring this topic? This article book some of these questions on interplanetary explorations, while also building an understanding of this project.

On October 1, 2022, We crossed a major milestone in our life. Our first serious mission, WIF, entered into our brain, putting the Students of Kendriya Vidyalaya in the same league as the other big schools and students of India, the only ones ever to have accomplished a similar feat.

We described WIF, and its journey, as a technology demonstrator mission and not so much as a science mission. India had never done it before. Technologically more advanced school and people, never thought about it. Flood is a tricky venture. Designing a trajectory for an eventual encounter with a natural disaster at a area of hundred kilometers is no minor task.

The fact that we are on a moving launch platform (the Cargo plane), with the target also moving relative to us, increases the complexity of the trajectory calculations involved.

CHAPTER TWO

Why Floods?

From the point of view of distance from our eyes, problems are closer than solutions. Why then did we pick up this topic ? There are two main reasons for this:

1. From a scientific exploration point of view, We shares more with peoplpeople in south than in north. Thus, it provides plenty of opportunities to understand the geological and biological processes that could have shaped the evolution of this places.

2. Compared to North, it is easier to gather information about the terrain and surface features of South Indian from a short distance as we live in south.

CHAPTER THREE

A Flood, sibling of the past

There have been notable recorded floods that have occurred in India. Floods are the most common natural disaster in India. The heaviest southwest, the Brahmaputra and other rivers distend their banks, often flooding surrounding areas.

Climate change is said to have in part caused (but may also be a natural evolution of earth's cycle) large-scale floods across central India, including the Mumbai floods of 2006 and 2017.

During 1901-2015, there has been a three-fold rise in widespread extreme rainfall events, across central and northern India – Gujarat, Maharashtra, Madhya Pradesh, Chhattisgarh, Telangana, Odisha, Jharkhand, Assam and parts of Western Ghats – Goa, north Karnataka and South Kerala.

The rising number of extreme rain events are attributed to an increase in the fluctuations of the monsoon westerly winds, due to increased warming in the Arabian Sea. This results in occasional surges of moisture transport from the Arabian Sea to the subcontinent, resulting in heavy rains lasting for 2–3 days, and spread over a region large enough to cause floods.

CHAPTER FOUR

The Plan And Idea Payloads

We require a vehicle, to propel and position the boxes into the desired places. The vehicles are usually airplanes. The Mission Water in floods will be launched on the Cargo plane.

A cargo aircraft (also known as freight aircraft, freighter, airlifter, or cargo jet) is a fixed-wing aircraft that is designed or converted for the carriage of cargo rather than passengers.

Such aircraft usually do not incorporate passenger amenities and generally feature one or more large doors for loading cargo. The box is enclosed in a floating material, a protective layer of several materials split into two halves that come together.

The object is none other than thermocol. Maybe weird to hear, but thermocol is the best option. As the airplane picks up momentum, the boxes hanging on the plane will automaticaly fall from the airplane and seperate from each other.

They will fall in 10m radius and every body will get it equally.

CHAPTER FIVE

The needs

Now, let's discuss the things which will mainly help for providing clean water in floods.

1.

Flexible Collapsible Silicone Water Bottle Expandable and Foldable with Snap Hook:(x8)

1. The modern and stylish Silicone bottle With a subtle modern and elegant looks. Foldable water bottle can reserve 500ml liquid with only 198g in weight. It can be folded from 9.8 inches to 5.5 inches in height. Collapsible and lightweight design makes you 50% easier to place, portable and storage, The attached Snap hook will hang the bottle with your bag, cycle, waist.

2. Stay hydrated with the silicon water bottle. This multipurpose water bottle can be folded/compressed up to $1/4^{th}$ of its original size.

3. Made of high quality silicone material this bottle is durable and lasts long. The flexible material makes it easy

for the user to expand/compress the water bottle as per the requirement.

4. Comes with a sturdy carabineer to attach to backpack, bicycle, etc. The wide mouth opening of the bottle makes it easy to fill in the water and also to clean it when required.

5. Features: BPA-free, Leak-Proof, Freezer Safe, Dishwasher Safe. Care Instructions: *Before use, please wash with normal boiling hot water, rinse and air out to dry. *Tighten the cap and cover when using it to avoid the liquid leakage when squeezing the bottle.

2. Lifestraw Plastic Personal Portable Water Purifier, 200Ml:

1. Filters up to 1000 liters (264 gallons) of water
2. Removes 99.99 percent of waterborne bacteria
3. Reduces turbidity, filtering down to 0.2 microns
4. Very high flow rate, easy to clean and very durable
5. Shelf life - 5 years when stored at room temperature; used worldwide in harsh conditions since 2005; award winning and internationally recognized (200ml)